Musical Instruments

Drums

By Nick Rebman

www.littlebluehousebooks.com

Copyright © 2023 by Little Blue House, Mendota Heights, MN 55120. All rights reserved. No part of this book may be reproduced or utilized in any form or by any means without written permission from the publisher.

Little Blue House is distributed by North Star Editions: sales@northstareditions.com | 888-417-0195

Produced for Little Blue House by Red Line Editorial.

Photographs ©: Shutterstock Images, cover, 4, 7, 8–9, 11, 12–13, 14–15, 16–17, 24 (top right), 24 (bottom left), 24 (bottom right); iStockphoto, 19, 20–21, 22–23, 24 (top left)

Library of Congress Control Number: 2022910617

ISBN
978-1-64619-698-2 (hardcover)
978-1-64619-730-9 (paperback)
978-1-64619-791-0 (ebook pdf)
978-1-64619-762-0 (hosted ebook)

Printed in the United States of America
Mankato, MN
012023

About the Author

Nick Rebman is a writer and editor who lives in Minnesota. He enjoys reading, walking his dog, and playing rock songs on his drum set.

Table of Contents

I Play the Drums **5**

Glossary **24**

Index **24**

I Play the Drums

I play the drums.

I like to make music.

I play the drums.

I use my sticks.

I play the drums.

I move my arms.

I play the drums.

I move my foot.

I play the drums.

I have a teacher.

I play the drums.

I learn to play a beat.

I play the drums.

I learn to read sheet music.

I play the drums.

I practice every day.

I play the drums.

I wear earplugs.

I play the drums.

I am in a band.

band

Glossary

band

sticks

earplug

teacher

Index

B
beat, 14

F
foot, 10

P
practice, 18

S
sheet music, 16